LEAD

FOR LIFE

7 Essentials for Upright & High-Impact Leadership

Paul Omojo Omaji

Copyright © 2015 Paul Omojo Omaji

National Library of Australia Cataloguing-in-Publication entry

Creator: Omaji, Paul, author.

Title: Lead For Life: 7 Essentials for Upright & High-Impact Leadership/Paul Omojo Omaji.

ISBN: 9780994290823 (paperback)

Notes: Includes bibliographical references and index.

Subjects: Leadership

Dewey Number: 303.34

Printed by Createspace, Amazon, USA

DEDICATION

To Exemplars of *Lead For Life* , Everywhere.

CONTENTS

ACKNOWLEDGMENTS

The help of many made this book possible.

I remain continually indebted to:

- All those who fanned the embers of leadership in me with <u>opportunities</u> and <u>acceptance</u> from my younger years through to secondary and high schools, and throughout my adult years at universities, professional bodies and workplaces across several continents.
- Friends (far and near) who lived a life of integrity, prayed for me, and in whose company I felt supported to discuss the brand of leadership presented in this book.
- My wife (Alice), our children (Ruth, Reuben, Timothy, & Tabitha) and their spouses, and our grandchildren (Cathrine, Joshua, Isaac, Elijah & Noah) who inspired and gave me zest for life.
- Those who provided comments on the manuscript, including Alice, my life partner.
- My parents (Mr & Mrs Omaji Akwu –

both now late) and siblings with whom I grew up securely to become a person embracing a worthy brand of leadership.

- The Most High Triune God - my Creator, Deliverer and Sustainer, who models the *lead for life* paradigm and makes me continually aspire higher and righter.

Introduction: Leadership scarcity

Towards the end of the 18th century the English poet, Samuel Taylor Coleridge, wrote *The Rhyme of the Ancient Mariner* in which the sailor lamented that there was "Water, water, everywhere, [but not a] drop to drink". Over 200 years later (now well into the 21st century), the thought about leadership conjures up a similarly gripping imagery.

There are rulers, position holders, organisational chiefs, or power wielders (military, civil, or religious) – call them the 'smart' ones - everywhere. Yet, leadership in general remains 'the scarcest resource in the world'. Worse still, the absence of <u>upright</u> and <u>high-impact</u> leadership (or what I characterized in another work as *leading right* (Omaji, 2015), is 'the pandemic of our time'.

Timothy Clark argued this point powerfully in his book, *The Leadership Test: Will You Pass?* There, he drew out the punch line: "we don't need more smart people. We have plenty of those. It's a poverty of principle we face, a crisis of character".

If you are reading this book, you are most probably one of those that are concerned about this situation. You are in good company. Some of us have been gripped by all this as well. If, on the other hand, you are merely curious, please read on. Curiosity is the engine of change.

I have marveled at the folly of rulers or position holders taking their entities (self, organisations, nations, etc) to the precipice if not inside of avoidable landfills ('death') when it is indeed quite possible to take them to worthy legacies ('life'). Surely, we don't all have to end up in landfills - with compromised destinies! Whether you end up with compromised destinies or fulfilled destinies depends on what you lead for – solely for yourself or for the collective. The allurement for a selfish focus is so great in the corrupt world. Yet, human beings are designed for a more noble end. This is what the history of leadership shows.

However, to post a flourishing destiny for individuals, organisations or nations especially in the corrupt world of today, we must look beyond the general leadership phenomenon. We must strategically seek those features that manifest upright discipline, dedication, and determination about a <u>cause</u> that goes far beyond our selfish interests and touches many lives positively.

This is the **lead for life** agenda that I set out in this book. If ever the world needed anything fundamental, with the ongoing challenging moral and resource circumstances, it is this agenda and it is now. You and I can make a positive high impact on this needy world – foremost of all, by learning to lead better and uprightly.

This book, *Lead for Life*, draws from my study and personal experiences to present seven of what I consider to be essentials precisely for such a desirable impact. In the rest of this introductory part, I have set out the backdrop that puts these essentials in a clear perspective, showing that it all comes down to the matter of character.

We need not go too far back into antiquity before we meet what Parker (2013) calls the "Failures of leadership: History's worst rulers and how their people suffered for it". The whole world has witnessed many a 'leader' who has ruined their own life and taken down their societies or organisations disastrously with them. No aspect of society has been spared this scourge. One or two illustrations from ancient and modern history will suffice.

Many mighty have fallen

Emperor Nero began his reign at the age of 17 and promised to return to the good principles of some of the previous Emperors. Indeed, he wanted to re-brand Rome as "a place of humanity and beauty, not violence". However, he ended up setting fire, fiddling and watching Rome burn. All the while, he was scapegoating, divorcing serially and murdering relatives and allies alike to sustain his power. By and large, the Roman Senate declared him a public enemy number one. He later committed suicide in 68AD.

Ivan Vasilyevich, who later became known as Ivan the Terrible, was the first Tsar of the nation (Dutchy of Moscow) that became Russia. He was under 20 when he assumed the leadership position and, in the next 51 years, expanded the nation by territorial acquisitions through conquest. He started well, demonstrating in the first few years, "a sudden and uncharacteristic commitment to morality. He was both transparent about and repentant for his former wrongs… [and] vowed to rule Russia justly…".

Then, there was a turn of events. He exhibited paranoia, loose living, and brutality. He created a personalized ruling elite which he allowed to "loot, rape, torture and kill". He "isolated himself from much of his empire"; and resorted to consolidating Russia (read, his power) "by any means necessary". His unenviable "legacy is indissolubly connected with the modern nation that descended from his [mis]rule", says Parker (op. cit).

Move from the political world of yesteryears to the business world of contemporary times. You would confront the Enron collapse in 2001 which is already legendary. This cost people their lives, thousands of their jobs, retirements, and many millions of dollars in investment. It stands till today as the ultimate tale of greed perpetrated by persons with character failures at the helm of organisations.

In a book with a fascinating title, *Why are we bad at picking good leaders?*, Cohn and Moran (2011) captured the shenanigans of Jeffery Skilling (the President of Enron) who brought his organization to ruins. Skilling could have been a famous 'leader' of our time. At age 44, he became the president of Enron which was then a Fortune 500 company[1].

He had an MBA from Harvard University. He was the intellectual horsepower - luminously brilliant and visionary; a paradigm changer, and an innovative thinker. He almost singlehandedly revolutionized the energy sector. Within 10 years, he lifted the market capitalization of Enron from $4billion to over $100billion.

Shortly before the storm broke over Enron, Skilling was reported to have claimed for Enron: "we are the good guys. We are on the side of angels." Suddenly, Enron ended up in a catastrophic bankruptcy. As Elkind and McLean (2003) observed,

> It was an event that sent shivers throughout the whole world. The subsequent unraveling of the truth would bring down CEOs, taint the President, destroy the accountants..., and call into question corporate governance throughout the US. It was the beginning of the end of confidence in American stakeholder capitalism.

Following the collapse of Enron, Skilling was

indicted on 35 counts of <u>fraud</u>, <u>insider trading</u>, and other crimes related to the Enron scandal. After so many legal maneuvers, this highly acclaimed captain of industry ended up with a 24-year prison sentence. Johnson (2003) summed up the underlying character failure rather graphically:

> Top officials at Enron abused their power and privileges, manipulated information, engaged in inconsistent treatment of internal and external constituencies, put their own interests above those of their employees and the public, and failed to exercise proper oversight or shoulder responsibility for ethical failings.

Less known, but similarly devastating as Enron, was the largest bank failure in history, namely the collapse of Washington Mutual.

This also happened under the watch of its Chief Executive, Kerry Killinger. In *The Lost Bank: The Story of Washington Mutual*, Kirsten Grind narrates how Killinger drove the bank to this debacle.

Barely a decade after he took over from the former Chief, Lou Pepper, Killinger was said to be 'on top of the world'. He had built Washington Mutual into 'a national superstar, capturing billions of dollars in deposits' and running extensive mortgage banking. In 2004, he earned the title the 'banker of the year' and was sought after as 'an expert on acquisitions' who had produced an 'extraordinary succession of record-breaking profits'. He was 'Alexander the Great' of the banking industry.

Underneath this glamour, however, this banking gladiator oversaw 'systematically inflated appraisals' and 'dangerously permissive underwriting standards'. The bank's mortgage business transformed into a 'culture of unmitigated greed' and, of course, Killinger's lifestyle had altered in synchrony.

Killinger, 'who once stripped companies of executive perks, was growing accustomed to them': e.g. using corporate jets for personal purposes at huge costs to Washington Mutual. His salary more than doubled into double digit millions in four years. Having gone headlong into the corporate fast lane, 'he became much more accustomed to the trappings of a CEO' with no scruples. Apart from the unethical private jet travels, Killinger was said to have relished in 'lavish homes…, and a big boost in executive compensation' for himself.

With such a lifestyle from the top, it was inevitable that so many faultlines would show up in the bank. When the crunch time came in 2008, the federal regulators marched into the bank's headquarters in Seattle, seized the bank (together with its huge assets of $307 billion), and turned them over to JP Morgan Chase for a paltry figure of $1.9 billion.

Killinger challenged Kristen Grind's story, shifting the blame to 'the financial industry's widespread failure to anticipate the housing collapse'. However, he was reported to have settled two lawsuits over the 'reckless lending' of Washington Mutual with hundreds of millions of dollars in payment. He has since lived a recluse life: 'Killinger, once one of America's most lauded bankers', has become a pariah.

A story was told about the death of one of Killinger's associates at Washington Mutual, Doug Wisdorf, who hanged himself about one year after the collapse of their bank. When Killinger turned up where his other colleagues had gathered to mourn this loss, 'people turned their backs to him. The chill was palpable'.

The Character Question

The most common factor among all these 'many mighty' who have fallen - position holders who have led themselves and their countries/organisations to ruin, is that they all displayed a high level of charisma but lacked character. For instance, after narrating the disastrous story of Jeffery Skilling of Enron, Cohn and Moran posed a pungent question: "what went wrong?" They were as resounding in their answer: "lack of integrity".

They make the point that without this foundation of integrity, people can lie, cheat, steal and, indeed, kill their way to the top and do same to remain there. In the process, they destroy themselves and their societies or organisations. The truth is, nobody can lead for life without this foundation of character in general and integrity in particular.

Why is this truth so fundamental? All other problems can be fixed while the rest of the building stands. However, the integrity problem which lies deep in the foundation cannot be fixed, except you bring down the whole house first. If the foundations be faulty, even the righteous will struggle to salvage the whole edifice intact.

Leaders need to live a life of virtues out of which comes integrity. They not only must be selfless, but they must also - at the core - be honest, prudent, courageous, self-controlled, and transcendent. They must lead uprightly even when others - counterparts or contemporaries - are taking shortcuts to get ahead.

Most probably, this would entail sacrifice – a sacrifice of security, comfort, health, etc. However, the sacrifice is nothing compared to the thrill of wearing the badge of honour that comes from leading for life and not death of others.

Look at Mother Teresa. This Albanian nun lived most of her life in India helping what she called, "the poorest of the poor." She sacrificed seeing her own family, the security of a convent, and the knowledge of where her next meal would come from to lead an organization of women who aided the sick, afflicted, hungry, and homeless. She gave selflessly, led uprightly and left a legacy (life) that carries on her mission to this day.

Mother Teresa knew the major toolkit needed for success as a leader. It's the same toolkit needed more for today's leader in an increasingly decadent and selfish world – the *lead for life* kit.

With leadership comes power and with power there is the temptation to take advantage of people, resources, and even opportunities for material possessions that may become available. What is it in power that corrupts easily and, in some cases, absolutely? I find the perspective of Aung San Suu Kyi, whom we'll meet later in Chapter 6, so illuminating: "It is not power that corrupt, but fear. Fear of losing power corrupts those who wield it..."

In contradistinction, upright leaders suffer no such fears; they can and will make the right choices and selflessly stick to the right vision of making a positive impact on the world in whatever sphere of life they find themselves. Sadly, there is the pandemic lack of this type of 'fearless' (right-based) leadership.

Concluding remarks

This 21st Century is already having its own fair share of this pandemic. In its first decade, we have seen some notable natural and man-made disasters in which nearly 1 million people have died. At the heart of the loss of these lives is the culpability of poor (fearful) leadership.

We owe to ourselves and the future

generations a duty to learn about, seek after, and enthrone the *lead for life* agenda. This is the aim of this book; and it is pursued by beaming a searchlight on this agenda and seeking to arm all of us with those <u>essentials</u> that can position us to shift the pandemic around.

These essentials are: the interest that looks beyond self; the picture of the future (vision) that is clearly defined; the principles (value-based moral rules) that serve as the correct compass for a successful leadership journey; the ownership of the vision that is shared to carry everyone along; the discipline of turning vision into reality; the consciousness of living on by way of positive legacy; and the sustenance of the dignity of oneself to the finishing line.

These essentials constitute the leadership

character required for this seemingly imponderable project. The book then concludes by drawing together all the major threads that run through the narrative.

---

[1] **Fortune 500** - list of corporations published annually by *Fortune* magazine ranking the top 500 U.S. companies in order of their gross revenue.

1 Interest - look beyond self

One of the foundational essentials for upright and high-impact leadership is a healthy appreciation of the notion of 'interest'. In a brilliant blog, Anne Murphy Paul (2013) makes the point that interest is a "psychological state of engagement", experienced in the moment, and also a predisposition to engage repeatedly with particular ideas, events, or objects over time.

Drawing on some university-based researches, Anne notes how interest acts as an 'approach urge': it "pulls us toward the new, the edgy, the exotic". It provides a sense of being energized and invigorated, captivated and enthralled. Interest has to do with what seizes the attention, stimulates the imagination, and reveals deeper meaning and purpose for one's existence.

Power of interest

In this regard, interest has the power to transform struggling performers, and to lift high achievers to a new plane for good or bad. It does this by pushing back against the "avoid urges" that would keep us in the realm of the safe and familiar, albeit non-productive, environments. However, this power can only serve the upright-leading for high-impact outcomes (i.e. *lead for life*) if it is deployed on the right things, <u>selflessly</u> or self-disinterestedly and not <u>selfishly</u>.

This is similar to Dr Adalat Khan's well-argued point on the place of faith (Arabic, 'Iman') in Islamic leadership. Although faith lays the foundation of greatness and success in, or is a quintessential for, leadership, it must be the one:

> grounded on good and righteous pillars and not bad and evil ones. There are people in fact thousands of them who believe [have faith] in evil, bad, irrational, and un-natural things. They may get whatever they wish to get but they are not great leaders, because great leaders have noble values and great missions and their faith and beliefs are based on all things right (Khan, n.d).

To *lead for life*, the leader must understand the fundamental difference between self-interestedness (good-directed faith) and selfishness (evil-directed faith), and take a stand for the former while actively rejecting the latter. If the 'approach urge' of interest pulls you toward the new, the edgy, the exotic so that you can exclusively be concerned about only yourself to the detriment of others, you are selfish.

Invariably, you would <u>not</u> care what you have to do to get what you want. Being preoccupied with 'what's in it for me', you develop a very low threshold (if any) for ethics, values, or virtues. In this state of mind, you lose the moral dimension that is so necessary to the *lead for life* project.

Conversely, if the 'approach urge' of interest pulls you to be concerned about your own well-being so that you can better still be of use to others as well, then you are selflessly self-interested. As Golden (2011) put,

> having a healthy self-interest doesn't preclude caring about others. Actually, a strong self-interest is a core component of those who are most concerned about other's welfare. If you don't care about yourself, how can you care about others?

In a training I did for some 300 'restive' youth in entrepreneurial civic responsibility and leadership, I distinguished between selfishness - as 'doing only what is good form me' from self-interest - as 'doing what is important to me, including being part of something larger than myself' (Omaji, 2009).

I also made the point that selfish service leads to self-destruction, drawing on Horace Mann's aphorism that "doing nothing for others is the undoing of one's self". On the other hand, selfless service leads to self-preservation: "we do ourselves the most good doing something for others".

In a healthy self-interest state of mind, you make choices not because they make you better off while others are screwed, but because your sense of being better off is intimately tied to other people's well-being. The following hypothetical aptly illustrates the key difference between self-interest and selfishness:

> ...a basketball player... needs one more point to be the all-time scoring

leader. It's his last game and if his team wins this game, they will be champions. They are down by 3 and there is 10 seconds remaining. If the player looks only for his own shot merely to get the scoring record, then he is acting selfishly. If, on the other hand, he passes the ball to open teammates with better shots than he has, potentially sacrificing [his individual] record for the better [victory] of the team, he is acting self-interestedly and not selfishly (Market Power, 2011).

No one can lead, let alone *lead for life*, unless he or she understands and comes into leadership with a strong appreciation and commitment to a healthy notion of interest that is driven to serve the collective. People with such mindsets see leadership as a 'calling' they have to obey in order to serve a purpose larger than their own narrow interest.

In another work, I discussed how this <u>intrinsic lack of selfish interest</u> is like:

> some kind of powerful, magnetic force; something one feels he or she is 'born' to be and/or to do. It is not about the pure expression of power, activism or heroism around certain causes or social values... It is not about a position, or standing in an exposed place.... Rather... [it] is the pattern of behavior or sequence of moments in which a person consistently steps into 'the space' to be counted or to solve [collective] problems in an upright manner (Omaji, 2015).

I further argued, in agreement with Oestreich

(2009), that this involves stepping out, stepping up, finding the rungs and handholds that enable a person, group, or global tribe, to find its way and know a truer compass to enduring greatness against the complexity and confusions of the world itself .

Selfless service

Unlike the 'smart' rulers who are attracted by positions and for whom the burden of public affairs must produce its own instant material reward, persons with a *lead for life* interest are drawn to the act of leading, sometimes, even with a sense of reluctance. There is no allurement from personal success, social rank, formal power, or instant gratification. Rather, the 'approach urge' is about making a difference - lifting up people and humanity.

Ultimately, it is ordinary people selflessly making extraordinary difference or, as the Christian Science Monitor puts it, "ordinary people taking action for extraordinary change" in other people's lives that produces high impact in all facets of life, including nation building and world peace.

Several examples abound. Take Ursula Cats, for instance. She is an anthropologist and drama therapist who went to do research in Myanmar (Burma) and Northern Thailand. During her work in Burma she met many women who were talented but poor, and stuck in traditional roles without a voice. These women cried out for empowerment. "The people there basically said what Aung San Suu Kyi said, 'Use your freedom to promote ours,'... I couldn't let go of the people asking me", says Cats (2014).

Being an advocate for human rights, with a healthy notion of interest, Cats founded *We Women Foundation*, to turn the lives of these women around. Operating from Chiang Mai, Thailand (because of the risk of political oppression inside Myanmar), the Foundation provides these women with access to higher education so that they could become leaders in their communities.

It empowers the women not only so they can make changes in their own lives, but also to make them a voice (agents of change) in their communities. Hence, their mission - as summed up in a slogan, 'educate one, empower thousands'. To date, the results have been remarkable: many women graduating from higher educational institutions and now helping to rebuild their communities and country.

Another ordinary person who took to making extraordinary difference, at a high personal cost, was Terrell 'Terray' Rogers. Terrell grew up in a tough part of San Francisco where he had gotten into some trouble a lot. He turned his life around and decided to dedicate himself to helping young people stay away from trouble (violence).

Terrell started a charitable work with young people in the same Bayview neighborhood of San Francisco, California where he grew up. He became known for solving problems in a community where "gun violence claims more lives than any other place in The City". He often was called to inner city schools to mediate disputes. He crusaded for peace on the streets and everywhere; and earned the title of a "beloved diplomat of the streets".

Having grown up in the tough part of the city, he knew what street life could lead to, but considered not his own life more important than that those of the city's youth. He did touch many lives, positively. While attending his daughter's basketball game in 2008, he was gunned down outside the venue. His cousin, Sean Robinson, bore him this testimony: "Terry knew what his eventual fate would be in this city, but he still kept his head on straight and did what he thought was right. His right was fixing everybody's wrongs".

Perhaps, we need to balance the narrative here with an example from among extraordinary people who have changed lives selflessly and extraordinarily as well. The person that comes readily to mind is Nelson Mandela of South Africa. Drawing on the "Tributes by world leaders"[2], I'll let the following excerpts do the narrative:

"We come carrying our sorrow for all of the ways that we have fallen short of the example that Madiba offered us; an example of integrity, of reconciliation, of leadership in the service of the people. ... So we thank God for Rolihlahla. We thank God that this man had the courage to learn and to grow" (Anglican Archbishop Emeritus Desmond Tutu and fellow winner of the Nobel Peace Prize).

"The world has lost a visionary leader, a courageous voice for justice, and a clear moral compass. By showing us that the path to freedom and human dignity lies in love, wisdom and compassion for one another, Nelson Mandela stands as an inspiration to us all" (Kofi Annan, Chair of The Elders).

"Today the world has lost one of its most important leaders and one of its finest human beings... History will remember Nelson Mandela as a champion for human dignity and freedom, for peace and reconciliation. We will remember him as a man of uncommon grace and compassion, for whom abandoning bitterness and embracing adversaries was not just a political strategy but a way of life...All of us are living in a better world because of the life that Madiba lived. He proved that there is freedom in forgiving, that a big heart is better than a closed mind, and that life's real victories must be shared" (Former USA President Bill Clinton).

"... And we have lost one of the most influential, courageous, and profoundly good human beings that any of us will share time with on this Earth. ..Through his fierce dignity and unbending will to sacrifice his own freedom for the freedom of others, Madiba transformed South Africa - and moved all of us…A free South Africa at peace with itself - that's an example to the world, and that's Madiba's legacy to the nation he loved… a man who took history in his hands, and bent the arc of the moral universe toward justice" (President Barack Obama, United States of America)

"President Mandela and his generation discovered the mission of their generation. They were at all times faithful to it, as a result of which they fulfilled it" (Former President Thabo Mbeki).

"A great light has gone out in the world… My heart goes out to his family - and to all in South Africa and around the world whose lives were changed through his courage" (United Kingdom Prime Minister David Cameron).

"Nelson Mandela was a wonderful man. He was wise, warm-hearted and humorous. ..Nelson Mandela was convinced that it is neither hatred nor vengeance that turn the world into a better place, but reconciliation and peaceful change... he is a giant of history, a statesman with a message resonating in all countries and for all times" (German Federal Chancellor Dr Angela Merkel).

"When history speaks of the very best examples of humanity, we will speak of Nelson Mandela. His life was dedicated to the greater good. He held strong beliefs and did not give up on his dreams. He was a driving force for change and cared for the well-being of others" (David Johnston, Governor General of Canada).

"Despite his long years of captivity, Mr. Mandela left prison with a heart closed to calls for a settling of scores. Instead, he was filled by a longing for truth and reconciliation, and for an understanding between all peoples. He demonstrated that the only path forward for the nation was to reject the appeal of bitterness. His forbearance was legendary: his magnanimity spared all South Africans incalculable suffering" (Stephen Harper, Prime Minister of Canada).

"… Dr. Mandela made unparalleled personal sacrifices. .. Dr. Mandela will always be remembered and honoured by all mankind as one of its greatest liberators, a wise, courageous and compassionate leader, and an icon of true democracy" (President of Nigeria Goodluck Jonathan).

"Nelson Mandela was a giant for justice and a down-to-earth human inspiration... He touched our lives in deeply personal ways... Nelson Mandela showed what is possible for our world and within each one of us... Mr. Mandela devoted his life to the service of his people and humanity, and he did so at great personal sacrifice..." (UN Secretary-General Ban Ki-moon).

"Go home Madiba, you have selflessly done all that is good, noble and honourable for God's people" (Cape Town Archbishop Thabo Makgoba, the Anglican Church of Southern Africa). "The imprint he left on our world is everlasting" (American civil rights leader Jesse Jackson).

Concluding remarks

When you consider the sketches I have presented here on Ursula Cats, Terry Rogers, and Nelson Mandela, what do you see that these people have in common? Regardless of the level at which each has operated, they are all leaders who understood and committed to interests in which they looked beyond themselves. Not only did they answer the leadership call; they did so with excellence, self-disinterestedly.

There is nothing to suggest that any of them was born a leader. All had to learn the role – starting by having to answer the call. They saw a need in their world and took the reins to make a positive difference, all the while holding their self-interest with the right perspective.

They didn't accept the position because it was vacant or that they saw a chance to make a lot of money. Rather, they gave sacrificially, taking on responsibilities at high personal costs, because they wanted to make a positive difference. They led for life for the people and motivated them to make their world a better place.

That is the kind of interest which shows up prominently in the foundation of those who *lead for life*: uprightly and with high positive impact.

---

2   See http://mandela.gov.za/quotes/index.html

2 Vision – see clearly

People do what people see. That is the law of the Picture.[3]

The eye is the lamp of the body... If then the light within you is darkness, how great is that darkness![4]

Vision is to leadership what eye (physical or inner) is to human living. Without it, the essence of leadership is diminished if not neutered, just like without eyes human living would be severely impaired. It is in vision that leadership finds purpose, direction, motivation, motion, focus, etc; and all of this helps the leader to drive high-impact performance and derive relevance.

Often defined as 'the mental picture of the future', vision may look simple. It is in fact as complicated and powerful as the human eye. In *On Origins of the Species*, Charles Darwin talked about the eye having "inimitable contrivances for adjusting the focus to different distances, for admitting different amounts of light, and for the correction of spherical and chromatic aberration".

This is basically observing how the complicated system of the human eye, consisting of some 40 separate components, can see only when these components work together perfectly[5]. Or, as Weed (2013) puts it,

> There's a lot going on in [the eye]... Right now, they're busy using all of that intricate machinery to refract and focus light from your... screen [or book pages] onto light sensitive rods and cones. From there, the light is being transduced into nerve signals, which are then being carried via your optic nerve into your visual cortex, where the raw information is getting filtered and patched together into something [a picture] that you can make sense of.

Vision is complex

Like the human eye, vision is complex. It's more than a value statement. It's not a fancy slogan that motivates an individual for a few seconds or even for a day. It's not what is made into a colorful poster that looks nice on an office wall. It's not something people forget about after the meeting. It's not "the statement" on top of the letter head or at the bottom of the page.

In vision's formation there is refraction, there is focusing, and there is channeling of data, information, knowledge, intelligence, and wisdom into an imagined future far higher and better than the current state of life in the visioner's eyes. Hence, if done properly, vision induces a compelling qualitative sense of getting from 'here to there'.

Vision is indeed the leaders' reason for being in office as such – to do what they do, motivate their teams to be the best they can and will ever be. It's the reason their organisation or nation exists and they are in the front leading.

If a vision is cloudy, it can be damaging for the individual, organisation or nation that is meant to make it happen. It is therefore imperative for the leader to see clearly the "imagined future", to clarify and to model the task inherent in the vision: "When the leaders show the way with the right actions, their followers copy them and succeed" (Maxwell, 2007).

As I have discussed elsewhere, this 'essential' is to do with seeing clearly, and giving meaning to, the vision with which the leader must set or establish direction and define the job to be done. It is a fundamental responsibility that must precede the other living dimensions of the *lead for life* project such as: aligning people through communicating the direction/job by words and deeds; creating teams and coalitions to understand the vision and accept its validity; and then motivating and inspiring them to get things done.

Andy Stanley put it this way: "Leaders can afford to be uncertain, but we cannot afford to be unclear. People will not follow fuzzy leadership."[6]

Icons of vision clarity

Charles de Gaulle - a French military general, they say, saw in 1936 the need for a military built on mobile tanks that were supported by aircraft. Though ridiculed for this vision, he persisted and took every opportunity to make it as clear to others as he had seen. Later, even his critics said this vision of a highly mobile and strong military presented de Gaulle as a man born before his time.

When the German invaded France in 1940, de Gaulle was asked to lead a tank division, which he did successfully with the needed air support of the French military just as he had seen prior. He eventually led his nation to being a free France and became its first post-World War II leader in 1945.

Lee Kuan Yew, the first Prime Minister of Singapore, brought that country from Third World to First World status in a single generation and stepped down after three decades in the leadership saddle. One of his weapons was vision clarity or, as former British Prime Minister Margaret Thatcher put it, "his way of penetrating the fog of propaganda and expressing with unique clarity the issues of our time and the way to tackle them"[7]. He visualized a decoupled (from Malaysia) and fledgling agrarian Singapore becoming a strong independent and industrialised multi-racially harmonious country.

With that focus, he led his team in industrializing, urbanizing, and educating the country. At the end of his leadership, Singapore was a self-assured independent Asian Tiger society with "a widely admired system of meritocratic, corruption-free and highly efficient government and civil service"[8].

Jack Welch became the youngest CEO of General Electrics (GE) in 1981. He had a vision that had been fine-tuned while working as a chemical engineer for the same company. Drawing on his unpleasant memories of bureaucratic red tape which he believed was inconsistent with the vision he had seen clearly, he streamlined GE's managerial processes. Welch taught and led his vision. During his tenure, the company's bottom line increased by 4,000 per cent. Welch had a clear vision and led by it.

Bill Gates and Paul Allen saw something that others did not see, articulated that "something" and built and managed those followers through the many changes called for by the vision. That's what they did with Microsoft. Steve Jobs and Steve Wozniak did a similar thing with Apple (see Gandz, 2009). Nelson Mandela saw clearly a positive vision of a racially harmonious South Africa, held it for 27 years extraordinarily in jail and helped bring it into reality peacefully when he was released from jail.

Vision is the driving force to which purpose is anchored. Leaders who have determined their visions clearly, know their goals for themselves and for their teams. They know where they are going and the purpose for being there. They know the influence or impact they and their teams will have on their communities in the course of pursuing the visions they have seen clearly.

For Bill Gates and Paul Allen, for instance, it was "computer on every desk". For Mandela, it was South Africa - a rainbow nation at peace with itself and the world. These leaders saw that impact from a far; they believed it; and they shared it with their teams. The world has never been the same.

Vision in harmony with virtues

A leader's vision not only has to be clear and capable of motivating people to be their very best. It also has to be pointing to a virtuous (honest, trustworthy, positive, etc) end for it to qualify as an essential for the *lead for life* agenda. It would not be susceptible or accommodating to cutting corners and taking shortcuts in pursuit of its goals. The *lead for life* vision must be above board and it must be aligned with virtues, key among which are wisdom, courage, justice, temperance (self-control), and transcendence (faith, hope, love).

Virtuousness, as I have argued elsewhere, is rooted in human character. There, it exercises to bring out what human beings ought to be: the inherent goodness, humanity's very best qualities and, ultimately, being in complete harmony with the will or purpose of God for one's life.

Therefore, a vision that is virtuous is one that is oriented towards <u>being</u> and <u>doing</u> good - not for selfish reasons but simply as an outward working of the inner intersection of the natural and the divine. Such a vision must be bigger than the leader – pointing to a greater impact on society. It must make a difference in the life of the immediate community and possibly beyond (Omaji, 2015).

George Washington, popularly known as the Father of America, saw that kind of vision for his country. It was a clear, thoughtful, and remarkably coherent vision of a fully developed constitutional American republic on a continental scale, "eager to promote [its ideal] wherever and whenever circumstance or the hand of Providence allowed". He saw this republic – led by people with personal as well as public virtue inextricably linked, enthroning the government of the people and "contributing to the uplifting and happiness in the years, even centuries, to come of the whole world".

His words – written or spoken – consistently revealed this vision. He maintained it throughout the three major junctures in the early history of the United States of America (US): the Revolution, the Constitutional Convention and the first Presidency that brought the US into being. At each of these junctures, he was **called upon to serve**; and he served from the vantage point of this virtue-compliant vision. In the nascent years of that country, Washington came to be seen as the indispensable man, the American Moses – a true hero with exemplary character (see Stazesky, 2000).

On a smaller scale, there is Wendy Kopp, founder and former CEO of Teach for America. While attending Princeton University, Kopp began discussing ways to improve the education experience for students attending the worst schools in America. Her vision included having some of the top college graduates volunteer to teach in these under-performing schools for two years.

Today Teach for America has expanded to include an international educational outreach organization, Teach for All. Kopp aligned her vision with the transcendental virtues of faith, hope and love to get to the is point.

Tegla Loroupe was a world-champion marathon runner from Kapenguria, Kenya, by all standards of her time and place. However, she was not satisfied with the personal success. She established the *Tegla Loroupe Peace Foundation* with a vision of "a peaceful, prosperous and just world in which sports is a unifying and livelihood factor".

The aim of the Foundation is "to become the leading international authority in the realm of conflict resolution and poverty reduction strategies... envisaging a lasting peace not only in the Sub Saharan Africa but also in other parts of the world wrecked and mutilated by conflicts". A key goal within this overly ambitious but other-focused vision is to dedicate "her track and field achievements, skills and friends to promote peaceful coexistence and socio-economic development of poor and marginalized pastoralists and agro-pastoralists: men, women and children in the Greater Horn of Africa".

Among several projects, the Foundation is building a school for orphans affected by the violence in the cattle raising areas of north-west <u>Kenya</u>, eastern <u>Uganda</u>, southern Ethiopia and southern <u>Sudan</u>. In 2006 the Foundation had sponsored its first long distance Peace Race bringing 2,000 warriors from six different tribes to the event. Loroupe virtuously uses her fame and the sport she excels in to amplify her vision for peace among the various warring tribes in her subregion.

There has been opposition even from close relatives, but Loroupe continues to live her vision of peace. She wants her message to endure long after she is gone, so she made peace with her father and she walks her talk each day among her people. And she slowly has gained their respect.

Vision succeeds with persistence

Not everyone will see your vision, especially if it's large and dramatic like the vision Washington had for America, de Gaulle for France or Loroupe for Kenya and beyond. If you actually believe in such a vision and not merely looking for a pretty poster slogan, then persistence is your friend. These leaders have exercised it for good; they did move forward with their visions despite oppositions.

For instance, Wendy Knopp was told graduates would not give up the two years of career building for such a challenge. However, she believed in her vision and was persistent. In 1990, 500 graduates signed up as the charter teachers for Teach for America and many more have since joined for the international scope. And, it is virtuously maintaining the vision at the forefront of your life like Loroupe that ensures nothing negative can be pinned to you or your leadership practices, even if said repeatedly by distractors.

Concluding remarks

Without vision people aimlessly wander around, bumping into each other and banging their heads on the wall. People perform tasks, but they have no meaning, no purpose, and feel there is not a reason to show up in the mornings.

For those committed to the *lead for life* agenda, vision gives purpose and meaning to everything they do as leaders. Vision sets the tone for each day and gives the energy to make it through its time. It is the key to motivate your team, especially as they see you living it out. Before that can happen, though, you must see this vision clearly and be able to explain the tasks inherent in it.

Without this, leadership is severely handicapped if not compromised. It will be easier to be open and honest about your leadership if it is about a virtuous vision. The story of how you came about it – whether it be through traumatic events, hardships, or life-changing encounters – may be regaling. However, it is the virtuousness (at the very least, selflessness) of both the vision and the life of its carrier that would stick.

Recall John Delorean who created the ultimate dream car for the rich in the 1980s. Almost unheard of in the auto industry, his cars held their value or increase in value. A pre-owned 1981 DeLorean car that originally sold for $25,000 can be found at an online shopping site for $54,000. DeLorean set the standard for excellence in an automobile. His dream was slick, stylish, and was wrapped in stainless steel. His car was a status symbol.

There was no shortage of partners and buyers for his vision – well, until he was caught in possession of a bag filled with drugs with a street value of $24 million. Even though DeLorean was later acquitted of all charges, he never could find the road to success again, as observers said. People did not want to associate with him because his vision had lost its ethics.

Once the integrity of the vision and its carrier is assured, and persistence is deployed in its implementation, you have a winning formula for an upright and high-impact leadership in a vision clearly seen and articulated.

---

3   See Maxwell (2007, p.158)

4   *Matthew 6: 22-23, Holy Bible, New International Version.*

5   "Irreducible complexity",
     http://www.darwinismrefuted.com/irreducible_complexity_02.html

6   Quoted in Maxwell (2007, p.160).

7   See http://en.wikipedia.org/wiki/Lee_Kuan_Yew.

8   There have been allegations of Lee corruptly fixing his family members into key positions. Lee went to court and successfully argued that those appointments were made on merit. E.g. the *International Herald Tribune* had to apologise in 2010 under threat of legal action that readers of one of its articles may 'infer that the younger Lee did not achieve his position through merit'.

3 Principles – hold your compass

Peter Drucker, a management guru, once said: "leadership is the lifting of a person's vision to high sights, the raising of a person's performance to a higher standard, the building of a personality beyond its normal limitations" (Drucker, 1974)

This is a powerful characterisation of leadership generally, and it has a particular resonance with a *lead for life* agenda. The compass (empowering software) essential for lifting visions, raising performance to higher standards, and building extraordinary personalities consists of values and principles. A leader of the mold of this agenda must establish his or her personal as well as organisational or national values and, then shift those values into principles in order to set a right directional compass.

From values to principles

Values are those beliefs about what the leaders and/or their organisations/nations consider important to themselves. As emotional standards, their impact resides mainly in their capacity to repulse people or draw them into instantaneous connection with the leaders/organisations/nations manifesting the values. However, like cloths, they can be put on and off rather whimsically, depending on the convenience. Herein lies the major weakness of values, even though they are very vital to leaders wishing to create a strong and engaging culture.

So, to make values more enduring, leaders must translate them into principles. In this format, they become moral rules (behavioural guidance) influencing or providing direction for actions or practice on a daily basis within the right-wrong framework. Covey (2003, p19) refers to correct principles as "compasses... [that] surface in the form of... norms, and teachings that uplift, ennoble, fulfill, empower, and inspire people". To bring out the distinction with values, he said: Hitler was driven by the value of unifying Germany, but that he violated compass principles and suffered the natural consequences, including "the dislocation of the entire world for years" (p95).

Establishing the empowering software as stated above is a major essential for the *lead for life* agenda. As the leader, it falls to you to design the environment that would involve the entire team in fashioning the software. Whether you adopt the in-house process or bring in external consultants to help, it is vital that all the members of the team get to participate one way or the other before the software is finalised.

Lead centrally

Having established the software, the leader must 'lead centrally' (from the front and all other angles) with the compass. Meeting your own standards is not an option for you, first and foremost; nor is it an option for the team in a *lead for life* agenda. There is little that is more disconcerting than for the leader to set the software and then behave rather inconsistently with that software. It's about walking the talk. It goes to credibility which gives you the right to ask others to follow you.

The ousted American Airlines CEO, Donald Carty, gives us one example. In 2003 the airline leadership was fighting with unions and asking its employees to make serious wage and benefit concessions to keep the airline in the air. And everyone came on board. The union and employees agreed to take the cuts so they could keep their jobs and hopefully avoid the painful bankruptcy where jobs definitely would be lost.

As the story goes, before the ink could even dry on the new concessions, Carty announced the company's new executive retention bonuses among other perks. That talk led to his disengagement and almost sent the airline into bankruptcy.

Conversely, the Chief Executive Officer of Southwest Airlines, Herb Kelleher, seems legendary with regard to setting and living out their strong organisational compass. In the airline industry noted for its formality and sternness, Kelleher led his team to set the values and principles as disclosed in their mission statement that are designed to make Southwest a very relaxed work environment and a business that connects leisurely with its customers. The elements of their mission statement include:

- dedication to the highest of customer service delivered with a sense of warmth, friendliness, individual pride, and company spirit;

- commitment to providing employees a stable work environment with equal opportunity for learning and personal growth.

- encouragement of creativity and innovation for improving the effectiveness of the Airlines;

- provision to employees the same concern, respect, and caring attitude within the organization that they are expected to share externally with every Southwest customer.

Kelleher has modelled this relaxed environment to the admiration of the entire Airline teams. Stories abound of Kelleher arriving 'at important board meetings on a Harley Davidson motorcycle wearing blue jeans and a plain t-shirt'; hosting bar-b-ques at 2 am for the mechanics on duty; holding larger company outings in unusual places, "such as one held on the deck of a U.S Navy aircraft carrier". Taking their cue from their leader, Southwest's employees enjoy comfortable work attire, team-building gatherings, and mutual-respect amongst all[9].

At Salem University

One of our first-hand experiences of holding the compass was at a private university that I led as the pioneer Vice Chancellor in Nigeria. A major challenge in that part of the world is lack of respect for time – either as a resource or as a framework for action. So, under my guidance, the Management team decided to establish values and principles around timeliness. Our commitment to modelling centrally or from the front on this issue was quite strong. In one of my addresses to the University community, I stated thus:

… Considering the change we must have,… and the excellence we must pursue in order to deliver on the vision mandate of the University, it looked as though we were running against time. As if that was not challenging enough, there was all around us a general disregard for time as a resource – totally oblivious to the fact that we do not control this resource. The entire environment with few exceptions was careless about, worse still averse to, timelines and timeliness…

No person can become an effective leader without having regard to time as a resource and a high sense of *timing* in what the person does. …

I harped on my conviction that the whole notion of 'time management' is misleading.

We do not , and cannot, manage time. Rather, we manage ourselves (in decisions, plans, activities, etc) in the continuous flow of time. Thus, we were sensitive about the timing of anything we needed to do, having bound ourselves to the mantra that effective leadership entails doing the right thing, the right way, **at the right time**, and for the right reasons.

For this reason, we worked hard to establish a University-wide consciousness about timeliness – for members of the University community and other stakeholders alike. Here is an example.

For the maiden matriculation ceremony of the University, we invited the Governor of the State as the special guest. Two weeks to the date, I went to his office and intimated his protocol team about our consciousness with timeliness. "At Salem University, our 10 o'clock is 10 o'clock; no African time", I informed the protocol. They said the Governor was comfortable with that.

A few days to the ceremony, we were informed that the Governor would be away and that he had asked his Deputy to stand in for him. Immediately, I went to the Deputy Governor's Office and intimated him and his protocol team about our attention to timeliness. Here again, we received validation for our time-related principle.

On the day of the matriculation, we were all ready to start the procession at 10 o'clock in the morning. The Deputy Governor had not arrived. I advised the Chancellor for us to start - consistent with our scheduled time. A few people around were apprehensive, wondering how the Deputy Governor might take it. My counsel prevailed and we started. … All those in attendance (the matriculating students, their parents, staff and other invitees) were deeply touched by our sticking to our scheduled time. This was a radical departure from the norm, especially when the programmes involved highly placed individuals. It helped to cement our resolve to enthrone timeliness in all that we did at the University (see Omaji, 2015 for fuller details).

Concluding remarks

Establishing the empowering software and modelling it as a leader is so essential in the *lead for life* agenda because, such moves help to build trust and confidence, foster accountability, establish a unified front, and provide guidance/steady frame in times of confusion, crisis or test of character.

Leaders who are not clear about the values and principles for which they truly stand:

> can never expect to lay a foundation for trust and credibility, let alone develop the capacity to exercise leadership... Through their daily choices [based on established values and principles], leaders carve out the character and reputation of [their] organization. In doing so they provide the standard by which others calibrate the appropriateness of their own behaviors (Friebergs, n.d.).

You will lift people's vision to high heights, raise their performance to a higher standard, and build their personalities to exemplary levels – in a phrase, lead for life - if you establish and hold (model, champion, etc) a correct compass of values and principles.

---

9   See MCO Group Management Consulting (n.a) "Assessing corporate culture: Southwest Airlines" Blog. https://murrayo.wordpress.com/ethics/assessing-corporate-culture-southwest-airlines/

4 Vision – make it their own

Vital as a healthy notion of interest, vision clarity, and the establish of a strong compass are to leadership (the points we made in the previous Chapters), unless your vision is shared by others, your leadership will still be shortchanged. Put simply, you must make your 'co-labourers' (followers and other leaders around you) own the vision as well, in order for your leadership to succeed.

This *lead for life* essential is about you doing what genuine leaders do to get these co-labourers, individually or as a team, to <u>buy into</u> their vision and/or that of the organisations they lead. By the time such leaders are done, the followers and other leaders around them are in the place or mindset where they would make the vision happen not because they are told to, but because they want to! How is that? Because it's their own now!

You must create a culture where these voluntary stakeholders (that's what co-labourers are) develop the sense of owning the vision. They see in the vision a stake to live and, if necessary, die for. There is such a level of engagement that these stakeholders look forward to coming to the organisation as a place of work, study or abode without the itchiness to run away at the slightest provocation.

It would be hard work for you as the leader to enact this essential. Your resilience will be tested in all directions. So also will your character, competence, and your focus on or commitment to leaving a lasting positive influence. If you pass these tests, you will gain the 'resonance' – a reservoir of positivity - that frees excellence (the best in your people) to manifest.

You will be regarded as the leader that moves his or her people, igniting their passion and inspiring the best in them through vision (yours or your interpretation of it), your powerful ideas, your participatory strategy, and your emotional intelligence. At this level, you have motivated and inspired or energised your people to overcome barriers and achieve results. Whatever change you introduce would be seen as useful changes that help every stakeholder to develop.

Creating ownership

Like music teachers, whom budding musicians follow and become great in their own right, the primary responsibility of leaders in creating vision ownership (or followership) is to <u>communicate well</u>. Music teachers can be 'friendly, chatty, and encouraging', but their efforts are geared towards passing on their own love of music. For this, they deploy narratives or story telling (which can convey instructions among other things), modeling and playing well.

Similarly, a *lead for life* leader can and indeed should deploy several strategies and techniques to communicate with a view to uprightly getting their people to understand and accept the vision of their entity. The right communication, in the right way, at the right time and for the right reason, will inspire acceptance, change, action and high impact.

First, fashion out the right message (clear vision) with its underpinning selflessness and software (values and principles) as outlined previously. Then, convey the message to your people - using 'melody lines'[10], imagery or symbolism, extrapolation (connecting past, present and future), and inspiration (common good), to make it their own. As Cohn and Moran (2011) rightly argued,

> all these methods must converge in a leader getting the vision to touch people's inner aspirations. It must

speak to their values and needs, and it must clearly explain the benefits of participating in a common journey.

This echoes an earlier conclusion from the analysis of nearly one million responses to a leadership assessment. That conclusion states that "what leaders struggle with most is communicating an image of the future that draws others in—that speaks to what others see and feel... [and is] able to bring their people into the future" (Kouzes and Posner, 2009).

Jesus Christ's IDEA (Instruction, Demonstration, Experience, and Assessment[11]) methodology, as John Maxwell discussed in his *Leadership Bible*, is a great example of communicating to create vision ownership. The Beatitude is full of melody lines. The parables, miracles and last supper are well suffused with imagery or symbolism. His teachings and preachings convey extrapolations all the way to the 'hereafter' and the common destiny that awaits those who buy into the message.

Results? He started with 12 men. Today, the followers (owners of the message/vision) number in billions. This is a strong evidence of vision ownership successfully created in an era when communication tools were very limited.

Mahatma Gandhi's 'liberation for India through non-violence' message or vision was shared through a similar communication approach. From "be the change you wish to see in the world" and many other 'melody lines', through his Charkha (home-spun cotton) attire, to the 240-mile march (the "Dandi March") performed in order to break the salt laws that required citizens to pay taxes when producing salt, and to fasting as self-control and self-denial, Gandhi enacted these elements of the 'law of buy-in'. And, he succeeded in getting his Indian people to own the vision of obtaining freedom without violence (see Jacobs, 2012).

Nelson Mandela, as we showed in the previous Chapter, is of this cast. At his trial in 1964, he stated his vision:

> I have cherished the idea of a democratic and free society in which all persons will live together in harmony and with equal opportunities. It is an ideal for which I hope to live and to see realized. But, my lord, if needs be, it is

an ideal for which I am prepared to die.

Twenty seven years later, he came out of prison and told his fellow Black Africans and their white colleagues that forgiveness was the most potent weapon to achieve the ideal he foresaw nearly three decades prior. And, with 'melody lines', symbolism, extrapolation, etc, he successfully communicated this vision and strategy. South Africa pulled back from the brink of full scale violence; and the blacks in particular, stepped away from a campaign of retaliatory genocide against whites.

At his inauguration as the first President of a democratic Republic of South Africa, he restated his vision with more vigour:

> We enter into a covenant, that we shall build a society in which all South Africans, both black and white, will be

able to walk tall without any fear in their hearts, assured of their inalienable right to human dignity: a rainbow nation, at peace with itself and the world.

Soon, the world saw him modeling racial reconciliation with the white Afrikaners when he publicly supported the predominantly white national rugby team; he took tea with Betsie Verwoerd, the widow of Hendrick Verwoerd, the chief architect of apartheid; and he stoicly avoided in words or deeds any African National Congress or Black African triumphalism (Campbell, 2013).

Passing it on in the daily grind

Ultimately, vision ownership is all about letting individuals within the entity know they are part of the vision designed to make a difference and that they are part of something bigger than any one person. Your communication must not only build their trust and encourage their input at whatever level of the entity they may be. It must also show that you know what you expect from them and that when they deliver, you would freely give recognition.

This calls for your ongoing interest in the daily grind of vision implementation. You must move among your staff and be visible in your recognition. Recognizing a job well done could be as simple as a 'thank you' and a handshake. It could mean a public thank you at the next group meeting. Or it could be free food or drink at lunch. Recognition does not have to be elaborate but it should be meaningful and noticeable.

The leadership at Google is illustrative. If there was a business that should have an excuse for not being able to recognize all its employees for their fine work, it would be this large company with its more than 28,000 employees spread out over 30 locations. But Forbes rates it as the best place to work. How come?

Google has a program called "Thank God It's Friday" (TGIF) where everyone gets together and employees are recognized through Google's 'recognition hub' called gThanks. New employees are introduced, company successes are announced, and employees are spotlighted and team work is rewarded. Bonuses are given for outstanding achievements. One office even started something as simple as a wall where 'thank you' notes and other kudos are displayed. It's evident that leadership takes charge at Google and rewards its team for their excellence. That is communicating to get 'buy-in' in relation to what Google stands for.

Using mistakes as learning opportunities can also be a powerful tool for vision ownership in the daily grind. As a *lead for life* leader you must expect mistakes and be flexible enough to capacity-build the culprits; and if necessary adjust goals to compensate for the unfortunate mishap while retaining the overall loyalty to the vision from the staff concerned.

One powerful way to encourage learning is to have the individual who made the blunder assist in the fix. Once the team member sees the vision, believes in it and is prepared to help fix his or her own let-down, then yelling and flying off the handle (even in their appropriate formats) would be uncalled for. Remember, your job is to encourage not discourage. Make them a part of the fix. Encourage them during the process and actually something good could come from the original let-down.

Look at Kellogg's cereal. Dr. John and Will Kellogg were looking for cheaper ways to feed their sanitarium patients. They had let some boiled wheat sit on the stove for too long and discovered it would tear and not hold shape. That was a significant let-down. However, the leadership mobilized all those involved to bake it and all the stakeholders liked what came out. Trying to improve the taste they switched to corn instead of the wheat. And that is how Corn Flakes came into existence. 'From ashes, a beautiful edifice can arise'.

So, just like looking at the big picture, you should look at all sides of the mistake and its fix and see if something better could come from the error. And then make the defaulting team member the resident expert on the fix or the new procedure. Have them teach others. Why? It allows you to foster ownership of the vision by giving the person who set back the vision the much needed prestige of becoming an 'expert' in fixing the mistake. And it teaches a team member a lesson in leadership. Part of communicating vision is through mentoring of those around you.

Above all, a *lead for life* leader must be visible in his or her own daily operationalisation of the organisational vision so as to enhance the buy-in by the followers. You don't need to be at the front; but be central. The Japanese communication culture in the work place conveys this point in their physical arrangements. In an office setting the leader's desk is placed in the center of the room to make him the focal point. In this setting, everyone can see the leader at work. The whole office knows what he is talking about.

Do not hide behind a closed door in your private office if you want to be a leader who fosters vision ownership, particularly in a new venture. When I was pioneering the building of a new university as the executive arrowhead, I adopted the 'lead centrally' approach to a significant success.

Occupying the central zone may be achieved simply by making the rounds – colloquially tagged "management by waka about". Talk with each member at least once in a fortnight or a month – depending on the size of your organization. Let them know personally how things are going and learn how they are doing. This is what we did among the units of the University in varying degrees. The community saw or felt our presence in its daily work.

Pope Francis is known as the pope of simplicity. He has avoided a lot of the trappings that come with the office of leading the Catholic Church. He chose a silver ring instead of the traditional gold when elected to office. He chose the guest house instead of the traditional plush apartment.

Critically, for vision ownership it would appear, he has chosen to be seen more in public in the poorer sections of cities where he can meet and talk with the "real people." Even though he now is the leader, he has not forgotten the team – the reason he chose to be a leader in the Catholic Church. He remains personable.

Concluding remarks

Where there is no vision, people perish[12]. The *lead for life* agenda is non-existent in that situation. The greater challenge with leadership is to communicate the vision so that the followers or the teams around the leader can see the vision as their own as well. It is the challenge of developing shared visions.

As one manager learnt from his direct reports, this is a deeply held view among followers. They said to him "You would benefit by helping us, as a team, to understand how you got to your vision. We want to walk with you while you create the goals and vision so we all get to the end vision together." (Kouzes and

Posner, 2013). Translation? 'Communicate to help us make the vision our own as well'.

In communicating to let the vision be their own, leaders should consider seriously the power of melody lines, imagery or symbolism, extrapolation, and inspiration in bringing the followers into the future with them. In this regard, Stephen Denning's *A Leader's Guide to Storytelling,* showing how storytelling can be used to spark action and get people to work together, would be an additional good resource.

You may set up special occasions to convey understanding of the vision to your team. However, it is imperative that you communicate and get buy-in from your team even in their daily routines; and your visible involvement will help greatly the achievement of the overall expected impact.

And when faux pas happens, be there to pick up the pieces and help the team put the plan back in motion. Even if it was a colossal blunder, make sure all disciplining is done in a constructive – not destructive - manner. Enough destruction happened with the botch so there is no need for an extra explosion from the leader. Use this time to rebuild the vision, and plan in the appropriate places to make it better and 'buyable'.

---

10 The line of rising and falling notes that gives a song its recognisable and memorable theme.

11 See John Maxwell's *Leadership Bible* for a more detailed outline of this methodology.

12 Proverbs 29: 18, Holy Bible. King James Version.

5 Reality – get it done

"Getting-It-Done Leadership". That is how Hybels (2002) called the essential of the *lead for life* agenda we characterise here as <u>turning vision into reality</u>. Bossidy and Charan (2002) bring out the sting in the tail – it is a discipline! That's what fascinated me about their book title: *Execution: the Discipline of Getting Things Done.* Those who have handled vision implementation before would know that this discipline requires shifting or going beyond the 'thinking through' into the 'follow through' paradigm.

Threshold test of rightness

Glorious as a vision may be, and remarkable as the selflessness, the software and the buy-in that underpin it may be, it is the decisions and actions leaders take to turn that vision into reality that ultimately determine how their leadership will be judged. The critical questions would be whether an edifice (a physical representation, a reality) is emerging from those decisions or actions and whether that edifice is fitting to the vision as seen and interpreted.

To answer the two questions in the affirmative, the threshold test for the *lead for life* agenda must be invoked: what is in the mind's eye (vision) must be the right thing, given a concrete expression in the right way, at the right time, and for the right reasons. No fabrication; no cutting of corners; no tardiness; and no dissimulation or Machiavellian obsession with 'the end justifies the means'. The what (end), the how (means), the when (time) and the why (reason) must all satisfy the test of rightness.

Enter the trenches

After this threshold has been reached, the leader should not pull out and hope that the system would work itself out to fulfill the vision. He or she must be up and about to give the necessary attention to his or her people and then guide them to actually make the vision happen. The leader must be seen to actually 'enter the trenches with the troops' and lead by example with a laser focus on delivering the right thing, in the right way, at the right time, and for the right reasons.

In all the places I have held responsibility roles, it has always been my standard that what I will not do, I will not ask my staff to do. As Geoffrey James has noted, one of the 10 Commandments of Leadership is "Thou shalt not ask an employee to do something that thou wouldst not do thyself" (#viii). That means, for instance that before I ask a staff to bend down and pick a scrap of litter that I perceive on the floor of a hallway and throw it into the trash, I must have done that myself previously or would do it when the situation arises.

Why is the ongoing involvement of the leader so critical to vision realization in a *lead for life* agenda? It is because every vision has its own specifications that must be met otherwise there will be no reality to it that is worthy of life. There are the 'engineering specification' where the edifice measures against the design work; the 'client requirements' where the edifice hits the technical points that make the reality of the vision adorable; the 'functional requirements' where the edifice matches the technical goal of the approval authorities; and, above all, the 'verification specification' where the edifice matches the core philosophy, mission and software (values/principles) that under-gird the vision.

It is the province of the leader to whom the vision has been committed to ensure that these specifications are met judiciously:

> vision is something that you need to
> keep alive. It is not enough that you lay

it out to your team in the beginning. It is important to remind them about it every day so they will not lose focus on what is important [or required] (Stanzma, 2014).

Also, turning vision into reality requires strategy, action planning and resourcing all of which again are within the remit of the leader to direct. Great visions are important, but all they are is talk without an execution plan. And plans are only as good as the people and the tools given to implement the said plan. To see the vision become reality you must walk the talk in front of the team on a daily or regular basis. To see it succeed you must guide the team through daily or regular input.

Illustration

The vision of the university we were tasked to

build was to make it "a center of excellence for the production of graduates who are worthy in learning and character <u>as well as sound in mind, body and spirit for outstanding leadership and global impact</u>". The first portion of being a centre of excellence is more or less generic in Nigeria. Almost all the Universities have that in their books.

It is the portion underlined that distinguishes the university of our assignment from *several* other universities in Nigeria insofar as I was aware at the time. That portion encapsulated the <u>daring to be different</u> of the vision. Quite significantly, it recognises the triune nature of human beings. Every human being has three parts (body, soul and spirit). Those who deny that turn themselves into animals - behaviourally, very easily.

We used the set of documents approved by the government regulatory bodies to draw out for the staff the conceptual roadmap showing the purpose of the University, where the University was, and where it was to go. Then, we set off with defining the task thoroughly, establishing the moral dimension (software), and deploying the strategies to get buy-in. Working within a very tight time-frame, we took on several fronts simultaneously, all the time guided by a sense of priority as to which governance, physical, and systems infrastructures were to be built, how, when and how.

Of course, consistent with strategic planning/action-plan design, we had to map out all broad areas of our responsibilities, define specific actions with timelines and figure out the resources required to get the works done. In the end, a university emerged from the dream and came to be recognised as such by all the key stakeholders. The "reality" (i.e. the edifice) satisfied the 'engineering specification' in our compliance with the University's design work. The main clients (parents and sponsors of the global leaders) found the reality adorable.

With 100 per cent accreditation by the main government regulatory body, National University Commission, we we knew the edifice also met the 'functional requirements'. And, the character transformation witnessed among the university community demonstrated that the edifice remarkably satisfied the 'verification specification' set out in the University's core philosophy, vision, mission and values. Such a reality could not have been achieved with just planning and resourcing. We (as the leader) had to adopt a hands-on (direct involvement or 'enter the trenches') approach among other strategies.

Leader visibility

As every *lead for life* agenda would demand, our visibility as the leaders was key. A leader must be visible (available and consistently so), in order to model the vision and monitor the temperature of its implementation. This becomes particularly essential if the vision to be turned into reality is about radical, or at the very least transformational, character changes as the one we implemented at Salem University was. Generally, people do what they see the model do. Greater is the influence if you lead them as a mentor which is a key pillar in a *lead for life* agenda.

From another level of educational

administration, we see also a down-to-earth illustration of leaders using direct involvement to actualise visions. Mr Baruti Kafele – a Principal at Newark Tech High School in Newark, New Jersey, utilised this approach with maximum positive impact. 85 per cent of students of the School were 'eligible for free or reduced-price lunch' at the time he took over leadership. That means the School was in a poor and highly disadvantaged neighborhood or community with a very poor completion (pass and graduation rates) record. Here is a summary of what Kafele did:

> "Good morning, good morning, good morning," the booming voice intones as students step off the bus and onto the school grounds. Principal Baruti Kafele extends his hand to and makes eye contact with every student as he or

she enters the building... Minutes later, over the public announcement system, he urges students to "have your best day yet while maintaining a positive attitude." Not content to sit behind his desk and push papers, Kafele stresses the importance of articulating a vision and then modeling that vision each day—during each classroom visit, each conversation with a staff member, and each discussion with a parent...

Principal Kafele's tall frame is often seen striding down the hallways of his school, from room to room, with the deliberate purpose of interacting with students. He explains, "You show me a school with a principal behind the desk, and I'll show you a school without principal leadership." The successful principal must be constantly "taking the pulse" of the school community...

Kafele ensures that he is constantly available to those with whom he works, particularly students: "his students have his cell phone number; they can call him 24 hours [a day], and that's really unheard of"...

Successful educational leaders build regular "touch points" into their day during which they consistently reach out to the school community. Kafele's touch points occur during students' arrival at the beginning of the day, morning announcements, and daily classroom visits... Members of the school community appreciate being able to count on seeing their leaders consistently... If a school's vision includes "growing together as a community," then the school leader must be an active presence and willing to build trust, share laughs, and interact in a meaningful way.

In the end, Kafele turned his vision of the School into reality: the community now have a School that "boasts a graduation rate of over 95 percent". Kafele was named a 2009 Milken National Educator. He credits his Schools' successes to his *vision* and his *visibility* (see Sterrett, 2011). The details of this approach are not as important as its inherent principle of visibility through involvement, and consistent availability in making vision a reality.

In the business world, we see Ray Kroc, the man behind the success of McDonalds using a similar approach. Kroc saw the McDonalds brothers' success and learned from their simplicity, focusing on a few things to create excellence. He bought their name and followed their pattern for quality. He then improved upon their plan by learning every step of the business process and improving those steps.

He developed Hamburger University so that franchise owners and managers could learn each and every step of the process so that no matter where a customer went, they received the same quality product. He demanded quality from the suppliers and implemented changes that improved their delivery process.

His story includes the point that even when

confined to a wheelchair in the final years of his life, he still went to work and called the managers at restaurants within sight of his office window reminding them to clean the parking lot and to turn the lights on at night. *Kroc gave daily input because he was involved in even the little things on a daily basis.*

Where innovation or adaptability is required to move things along, the active presence of the leader makes things a whole lot easier – especially if the time dimension of the yardstick is of essence. Put starkly, there is no room for 'absentee landordism' in the *lead for life* agenda. It's about <u>presence</u> that facilitates or nurtures growth and not just communicates or gives information.

Concluding remarks

Seeing your vision become a reality is exciting.

It's a little overwhelming at times – but it's exciting. To see it take shape you must give your team the clarity, software, and tools to implement your vision. If you go cheap in these areas then your team will lose their faith in the vision. They will become frustrated and you will not get 100 percent of their efforts. You must invest in the best to receive the best. So give your team more than a "broom" and you will have a sweeping success.

Also, you must give daily or regular input. Monitor, communicate, and facilitate; monitor, communicate, and facilitate; and repeat the cycle; and then again, and again. That is a sure way to see your vision completed and all goals met. It's that simple and it's that difficult. It can be tiring and at times frustrating. There will be moments when you think your team does not get it and the next moment they have surpassed all your expectations. Expect that because that is reality. That is part of the roller coaster ride called leadership. But you must give them constant feedback and encouragement to see the vision grow and become a reality. Your visibility is a sine qua non for this outcome.

6 Legacy – live on

*Blessed are those whose strength is in you
(God), who have set their hearts on pilgrimage.
As they pass through the valley of Baca
(Weeping), they make it a place of springs...*[13]

There is a gem of truth in the saying that if
you work only for a living, you are a labourer;
but if you work for legacy, you are a leader.
The *lead for life* agenda demand legacy-workers,
not mere labourers.

Fingerprints, footprints, visionprints

From a plethora of definitions of legacy, I find the one by a High School student quite interesting for its simplicity and imaginativeness. He said: "Legacy is the permanent and vivid fingerprint that a leader leaves behind. That legacy can mean anything - which gives an idea of who that person was and what they intended to put forth into the world" (Michael Shimek, Crawford High School, Nebraska)[14]

In the *lead for life* agenda, only those who work for a positive legacy can position themselves for upright and high-impact leadership. Their story would always be that they passed through a place and changed it for good. The change that qualifies for such a story, as I argued in another work (Omaji, 2015), is about leaving *footprints* (better still, *visionprints*) not merely 'in the sands of time', but *in the hearts of people*.

Footprints in the sands of time are momentous, no doubt[15]. However, to turn Baca (denoting wickedness, corruption, distress and weeping) into "a place of springs" (denoting goodness, integrity and joy), the audacity of the processes must necessarily result in something more enduring than the sands of time can bear.

On this level, your decisions and actions are in the direction of transforming (better still, transfiguring) the whole person, communities, organisations, nations, etc. into something not just better but beautiful. You make "the sky more beautiful to gaze upon". And, you *live on* in these lives for a long time, to the end that they are never ever the same again. This is a *lead for life* legacy par excellence.

Legacy prayer

Leaders with this kind of legacy interest or magnetic force in their hearts would pray like Dave Kraft who wrote *Leaders Who Last* (2010) did:

> Lord, make me a person who leaves footprints in people's lives. I don't want to be a person who comes and goes with no lasting impact. Because of contact with me, may people never be the same again. May I be a person who intentionally and lastingly influences others.

With such a prayer as an object of ongoing meditation, you will transform and become an asset of immense proportion in our broken and decaying world. It's all about adding value to others; and you must have resolved to distinguish yourself in doing so and lived your life like it is a book of goodness memorial: "Once the word *finis* must be written, let it then be said of your book that it is a record of noble purpose, generous service, and work well-done[16].

The world has had its own fair share of the worst or most insane rulers who have bequeathed destructive legacies to their generations and subsequent ones. We profiled a sample of these in the Introduction of this book. By the same token, the world has also witnessed some persons with a noble and generous pedigree as you would have noticed already.

In one of the research-based projects undertaken by the National History Day (NHD) - a non-profit education organization in College Park, MD, 100 most significant leaders (negative and positive) in the known history of the world were identified, covering the period from 4000 BCE to the present day. They were judged to be among the first 100 on the basis of how they articulated visions, motivated others, made effective decisions, confronted tough issues, and impacted history.

Noble and generous pedigree

Among them are several *lead for life* candidates. Those are leaders who have been internationally acknowledged as positive legacy carriers. To profile some in this book, I examined the eight out of the 100 that have ever won the Nobel Peace Prizes. Of course, this introduces a bias in favour of those carriers who bequeathed their legacies after 1900 when the prizes kicked off.

With this limitation in mind, I've summarised here the credentials of a couple of these positive legacy-carriers that the NHD considered[17]. The idea is to show how some of the *lead for life* leaders have left powerful visionprints in the hearts of humanity.

The first of the eight, Dr. Martin Luther King, Jr., won the Noble Peace Prize in 1964, attesting his influential and inspiring role as a charismatic, nonviolent leader. He was a leader in the Civil Rights Movement; and drawing from his Christian upbringing and the words of Mahatma Gandhi, Dr. King led by example and inspired millions to take part in a crusade to end legal segregation. His activism revolutionized the social fabric of America.

For Dr King, "injustice anywhere is a threat to justice everywhere". Against the backdrop of centuries of intense racial injustice and inequality - with public authorities upholding segregation in schools, housing, work places, stores, restaurants, public space, mass transit, sidewalks and drinking fountains, the environment in which Dr. King stepped out to be counted was most inhospitable.

It was no surprise that he was severally beaten, arrested, even stabbed, and eventually murdered. He could not be dissuaded from a just and value-adding cause. His convictions and actions have impacted the lives of millions. A symbol for hope, King still stands as a source of inspiration, and a model for social reform. The impact of King's social activism is evident today everywhere. The naming of a national holiday and numerous locations in his honour are just a few symbols.

On the other side of the globe, there is Aung San Suu Kyi – the only female of the eight Nobel Peace awardees. She won the Prize in 1991 and she remains a symbol of the fight for human rights and democracy in Myanmar. At a time when many would keep away or lie low in a faraway western country, Suu Kyi returned to her country after 20 years of absence and became the most visible individual in the opposition to Myanmar's repressive government.

Like Gandhi and Dr King before her, Suu Kyi led a movement focused on non-violence and democratic change despite the cruel repression by her government. Even when she had the opportunity to escape to the relative safety of the western countries, she chose to risk her life to make others free. Her 'melody line' on power and fear stands till today as a radical redefinition of the corruption from power:

> It is not power that corrupt, but fear. Fear of losing power corrupts those who wield it and fear of the scourge of power corrupts those who are subject to it ("Freedom from Fear", 1991).

The fact that her own father, General Aung San, had been assassinated previously for challenging bad government did not deter Suu Kyi from stepping out to unify the protestors fighting for basic human rights and representative government. Arrests that culminated in her being kept under house arrest for 11 years did little to make her pull back as a leader of the non-violent protest.

Like the great *lead for life* personalities before her, Suu Kyi has kept fighting for freedom at great personal sacrifice. That democracy is currently obtainable in Myanmar and, indeed, Suu Kyi winning election and serving as the leader of the National League for Democracy (NLD) in Myanmar's House of Representatives, is a testament to her commitment to a cause far higher than her own selfish interest.

While I was hiding away to finish the draft of this book in Kirribili, one of the leafy old suburbs of Sydney (Australia), I came out one morning and was confronted by this headline in one of the newspapers: "Malcolm Fraser 1930-2015 – A TOWERING LEGACY. He rose to Australia's highest office in one of the country's most controversial episodes, but Malcolm Fraser ensured he left a lasting mark on the nation as its 22 prime minister"[18].

This was how the death of Mr Fraser was captured in that paper. In some of the tributes carried by the paper, we find what this Prime Minister 'put forth into the world':

> "Malcolm Fraser held true to the belief that his actions were in the best interest of Australia. He was determined to turn on the lights and restore Australia's fortunes" (current Prime Minister Tony Abbott).

> "Prime Minister Fraser will be remembered as a compassionate Australian, who cared for people at home or abroad, who had little or nothing to

protect [themselves]" (former Prime Minister Kevin Rudd).

"Malcolm Fraser and I were on opposing side of the political fence. But I want to say at the outset that I had an absolute unqualified respect and admiration for one particular aspect of the political career of Malcolm Fraser and that was he was impeccable on the questions of race and colour" (former Prime Minister Bob Hawke).

"As Prime Minister, Malcolm Fraser showed international leadership of great integrity in condemning the evil of apartheid. He immeasurably enriched Australia's multicultural society, offering refuge to tens of thousands of vulnerable people driven from Vietnam by the horror of war" (current opposition leader Bill Shorten).

Malcolm Fraser attained notoriety when he was associated with the dismissal of a sitting Prime Minister (Gough Whitlam) which saw him becoming the Prime Minister. Years later (after he left office) he was known to have shown audacity when he turned on his political party "in his pursuit of human rights advocacy"; he resigned his membership of the Liberal Party, accusing it of lurching too far to the right on issues including the treatment of refugees.

At the community level, the President of the Vietnamese community in Sydney paid their own tribute to Fraser: "This is the saddest news to the Vietnamese community in Australia. Mr Fraser was the first person to act according to his heart and allowed the first wave of Vietnamese refugees into Australia after the war. [We] are in debt to his generous support and vision for a multicultural society".

Leader of leaders

Legacy attains its apogee when a leader raises other leaders to impact their own world far better than the one who raised them. Addressing the Law of Legacy, John Maxwell had this to say about himself:

> I have finally settled on the life sentence[19] that I believe will serve me the rest of my days. When they hold my funeral, I hope I will have lived a life that prompts people to know why I was here and they won't have to guess at it. My life sentence is, 'I want to add

value to leaders who would multiply value to others (2007, pp258-9).

Only a leader of leaders sets a goal of raising or value-adding to other leaders (not just followers). This is another strong component of the positive legacy as an essential factor in the *lead for life* agenda.

Not too long ago, I attended at Idah in Nigeria the funeral service of one of my prominent Igala tribesmen - a world-renown Nigerian professor of agricultural economics, Professor Francis Idachaba. I sat there watching many high-level leaders in different fields of life (academics, politics, church, farming, public service, etc) trouping out one after the other, and pouring glowing tributes about how Professor Idachaba had changed their lives for good.

At my turn, I stepped to the podium to speak. I established my connection with Professor Idachaba and my regret that we narrowly missed what turned out to be the last appointment to meet in Abuja before his travel to the US where he passed on (because he was delayed at the Presidency to where he had gone for a meeting that day). Then I said that indeed I hadn't come to mourn but to celebrate him as a <u>leader of leaders</u> (the tributes before my own already attested to that fact of him being a leader of leaders).

I said, the power of a leader does not reside in the number of followers he or she is able to mobilise in life. Rather, the power of a leader resides in the number of other leaders he or she had raised. I turned to the politicians in the hall and said something to this effect: unlike politics, leadership is not a popularity contest; that, if all the politicians can do is amass followers and keep them as such throughout their tenure in 'power', then they have not value added much; they have failed a key leadership test.

Finally, I challenged all of us to borrow a leaf from Professor Idachaba and produce many more leaders in our lifetime. There is no better way to lead for life and live on!

This is about 'developing the leaders around you'. It is about empowering others to make a notably positive difference in the world around them. You inspire them to learn and work individually and as a team to accomplish great things with high impact far above the dictates of their own immediate or selfish interests.

People who exhibit this 'leader of leaders' mindset are in the league that Collins (2001) called the 'Level 5 Leaders'. These leaders deliver superlative performances to make good companies or societies become great. They are self-confident enough to set up their successors for success. Humility (not hubris), mixed with a strong commitment to professionalism, is also a key characteristic of theirs. So also are: unwavering resolve, workmanlike diligence (more plowhorse than showhorse), and sharing of 'recognition stage' especially in times of success or good results.

Mo Ibrahim - African leadership

These characteristics apply with equal, if not more, force to the building of communities, nations, and continents. Take the Mo Ibrahim Award for Achievement in African Leadership, for instance. Established by the

Mo Ibrahim Foundation in 2007 to celebrate excellence in African leadership, the Award is an annual prize (bigger in monetary value than the Nobel Peace Award) awarded to a former African Head of State or Government who has satisfied specified criteria.

The closer I look at the criteria for selection for this Award, the more I see the Award mirroring a search for 'leader of leaders' in Africa. Essentially, the Foundation is looking for leaders who have developed their countries, lifted their people out of poverty, paved the way for sustainable and equitable prosperity for their people, and shown exceptional role models for the African Continent.

Notably, in this regard, the Award is directed at ensuring that Africa continues to benefit from the experiences and expertise of these exceptional leaders when they leave national office, by enabling them to continue in other public roles on the Continent.

Since the Award was launched in 2007, there have been four recipients: Joaquim Chissano, the former president of Mozambique (2007); Festus Mogae, former president of Botswana (2008); Pedro Verona Pires, former president of Cape Verde (2011); and Hifikepunye Pohamba, former president of Namibia (2014).

All of them distinguished themselves by governing their countries well. The areas where they made relatively extraordinary achievements include peace, reconciliation, national cohesion, stable democracy, commitment to the rule of law, tackling pandemics (e.g. HIV/AIDS), gender equality, sound public management, economic progress (including diversification), sustainable development (with strong investment in health and education, overall dedication to the service/safety of their people and/or vibrant international representations. They did all this, while retaining their humility and personal integrity.

Among the profound displays of their 'leader of leaders' quality is their voluntary stepping down from office at the end of their tenure and supporting their successors to stabilise. Chissano stepped down "without seeking the third term the constitution allowed". Pires stepped down at the end of his second term, dismissing outright suggestions that the constitution could be altered to allow him to stand again: "This is a simple matter of faithfulness to the documents that guide a state of law", he retorted!

Against the backdrop of the sit-tight rulership on the African Continent, as I'll highlight in the nex Chapter, this is demonstrative of leaders who recognise that there are other leaders who should be given a chance to develop and serve[20].

Concluding remarks

The simple but imaginative definition by the High School student, Shimek, of <u>legacy</u> as the permanent and vivid fingerprint of who leaders are and what they intend to put forth into the world underlines the power of legacy as one of the essentials of the *lead for life* agenda. Those who pass through the metaphoric valley of Baca and make it a place of springs clearly present themselves as *lead for life* personalities.

The high impact of such leaders is not mere accidental colossal collision. There is intentionality and there is methodism about what they do, how, when and why they do it so that it invariably results in changing the lives of individuals, communities, organisations, nations, continents or the world at large in a positive way. It's uplifting and/or bettering humanity's existence.

These leaders look past the now. They look at the future, not just of their own individual or family convenience but that of the entire entity they lead. Their decisions and actions are in the direction of transforming and indeed transfiguring humanity into something beautiful. Along the way, they raise other leaders who can multiply the value-adding impact in their own world.

The legacy of the type inherent in this *lead for life* agenda is costly. It involves high sacrifices: sometimes of privacy, comfort, health, and/or ultimately the personal life of the leader. The quintessence of this kind of leadership is that the leader does what Jesus Christ said about his own sacrifice: "I am the good shepherd: the good shepherd lays down his life for the sheep"[21].

---

13 Psalm 84: 5-6, Holy Bible, New International Version.

14 At
https://www.illinois.gov/ihpa/Involved/Students/Documents/20
15DefiningLeadershipLegacy.pdf

15   Indeed, almost all the literature of note on leadership counsel
people with such responsibilities to ultimately 'leave their footprints
in the sands of time'.

16 Glenville Kleiser in his book, *Training for Power and Leadership* -
quoted in Maxwell (2007, p259).

17 Check http://100leaders.org/ for more details about these

leaderhsip luminaries.

[18] *The Daily Telegraph*, Saturday March 21, 2015; front page.

19   A statement summarizing the goal and purpose of his life.

20 For details of these Awardees and their specific achievements for their countries for which they were recognised, visit the Prize subpage of the website of the Mo Ibrahim Foundation: http://www.moibrahimfoundation.org/ibrahim-prize/

21   John 10:11, Holy Bible. King James Version.

7 Dignity - Finish well

Whatever has a beginning must have an end. Considering the level of sacrifice involved in carrying the responsibilities of genuine leadership, it is difficult to fathom why anyone would wish to remain there for so long.

In fact, as the Prophet of Isam (pbuh) was quoted to have warned people seeking especially public office, "public office is a trust, a source of lamentation and remorse on the Day of Judgment"[22]. Such a burden compounds the mystery about the reasons for those 'sit-tight' rulers holding unto power – in some cases, until death 'do them part'!

The first 40 of such rulers in the world who made it into the 21st century have had periods ranging from11 to 42 years in power. At least 20 of them are found in Africa, most at the upper end of the time span[23], and three of them were swept away in the revolts or uprisings euphemistically called the 'Arab Spring'.

The 'Arab Spring' for me represented, principally, a commentary on <u>how not to finish</u> one's leadership. In recent times, there was Laurent Gbagbo, President of Côte d'Ivoire from 2000 until his arrest in April 2011, who was alleged to have refused to accept defeat in the polls and consequently plunged his country into chaos. Of course, this earned him the unenviable record of being extradited and becoming the first head of state to be taken into the custody of the International Criminal Court.

So, when Dr Goodluck Jonathan, a sitting President of Nigeria for six years, conceded defeat in a presidential election which was held on 28 March 2015, the reactions of commendation were staggering. Many dubbed it the first ever in Africa and were emphatic that Dr Jonathan, by that singular act, had transmuted into a statesman and written his name in gold forever. Needless to say, this was a welcome development, and probably with one more step (a critical one at that) it can indeed come within the finishing well framework in the *lead for life* agenda.

Home in dignity

There are three fundamental facets of finishing well in this agenda that I would highlight here: know your cause, respect your timelines, and maintain your credibility to the end. Supported by the right attitudes, principles, and practical actions, these facets will bring you home in dignity.

I am captivated by those who – having run their leadership race so well (with regard to causes and timelines), stand face to face with their community and proclaim their dignity (with their credibility in tact) without any fear of contradiction. Let me illustrate with two personalities, both of whom coming from the religious sphere were well aware of the divine consequences of any flippancy.

Samuel Elkanah, a leader of ancient Israel, received his calling to leadership (as Judge and Prophet) at the age of 12. In his 30s, he led Israel in successful wars against oppression and held the nation to a high standard of accountability to their God. Before he died at age 52, he summoned the nation to a valedictory (farewell) speech where he said to all Israel:

> As for me, I am old and gray, and my sons are here with you. I have been your leader from my youth until this day. Here I stand. Testify against me in the presence of the LORD and his anointed. Whose ox have I taken? Whose donkey have I taken? Whom have I cheated? Whom

have I oppressed? From whose hand have I accepted a bribe to make me shut my eyes? If I have done any of these things, I will make it right.

The nation replied: "You have not cheated or oppressed us. You have not taken anything from anyone's hand."[24]

Similarly, the greatest leader of Islam and the Muslim world, Prophet Muhammad (pbuh) started with a leadership calling (vision or series of revelations) in Mecca at a very early age. His 'seerah' (Arabic word for 'a way of life'), it is argued, demonstrated altruistic leadership principles. From a handful of individuals, the Prophet raised a very large and rapidly growing following even to this day.

Strikingly, when he died at age 62, he ended his leadership in dignity. Several writers acknowledge that the Prophet displayed humility and magnanimity in bidding farewell to his community after more than 30 years of sacrifice on their behalf. In his last speech in the mosque in Medina, given on the day he died, he is quoted to have said:

> If there is any man whose honour I might have injured, here I am to answer for it. If I have unjustifiably inflicted bodily harm on anyone, I present myself for retribution. If I owe anything to anyone, here is my property and he may help himself to it… Nobody should say: 'I fear enmity and rancor of the Messenger of God.' I nurse no grudge towards anyone. These things are repugnant to my nature

and temperament. I abhor them so (Toronto, 2000).

Back to the land of mere mortals and the case earlier mentioned, the decorum with which Dr Jonathan conceded defeat and called to congratulate the President-Elect, General Muhammad Buhari, clearly set a very high benchmark in a continent notorious for the grip of its sit-tight rulers. To complete the fundamentals for finishing well, however, leaders rounding up their tenures should consider the ultimate dignity in accountability as exemplified above in the lives of the two men of God.

Experience at Salem University

Three and a half years into my role as pioneer Vice Chancellor of the University (still four and half years away from the legally allowable end of my eligibility), I began to notice some restlessness in myself. Initially, I thought it was the usual weariness that comes to test one's fortitude after carrying a heavy pioneering responsibility for sometimes.

Yes, by this time, I had suffered near-death health challenges on two occasions, lasting about 10 weeks in total and pulling through both only by a whisker (more appropriately, the grace of God). All the while, with the exception of the few matters that I could delegate which I did, I was running the core affairs of the University - most of the time lying flat on my back.

Such was the grip of the vision of the University on our souls, that we thought less of the resulting impact on our personal health. To this high cost, you add having to manage the machinations of faceless saboteurs who preferred a leadership with which they could establish unholy alliances for their personal gain – at the expense of the unique vision of the University, and you can sense the level of burden involved.

If at that organizational level the burden of service could be, and indeed, was this heavy, surely it must be multiplied several times over at the national or continental level. There must be something that more than meets the eye which would lure people into a sit-tight power mentality to hang unto a responsibility that can potentially end your life with an awful reputation or taste.

Anyway, by and large, I received intuitively a clear instruction as to how much time I had left to lead the building of the University:

"You have one and a half more years at Salem University. And, I will be done with your frontline leading role *there*" (see Omaji, 2015 for more details).

I knew my timeline with the University had been drawn! I continued with my services as usual, still focused on the cause that took me there in the first place. The only different thing for me was I now had my eyes on a more clearly defined finishing line, but the integrity and intensity with which I discharged my responsibilities did not diminish. Rather, there was a greater sense of urgency in my steps and a renewed drive to finish well whatever needed to be done.

Locate this attitude in an environment where academicians would 'kill'25 to become Vice Chancellors or remain in that position, then you can appreciate why some people would disbelieve that I was intended on leaving within the new timeline. I made sure then, that my decision was put beyond any shadow of doubt by conveying my decision in writing to my employer. This happened about nine months before we got to the end of the new timeline.

When the time came - and despite letters of commendation for excellent leadership and of reappointment for a second tenure, and many counsel including from some of my fellow Vice Chancellors for me to stay on and enjoy the 'fruit of my labour', I vacated the position. This action surprised many, but not me.

I came to the Vice Chancellor position in the first instance as an act of obedience to a calling for a specific assignment. I knew my cause: to lead the laying of a strong and notable Godly foundation for a University that was envisioned to do something unique in the blighted and troubled educational/moral firmaments in Nigeria. That cause had been fulfilled. So, why linger a day longer?

Yes, as at the time the endpoint came, I had no other job to go to. The next thing in store for me was still very hazy. So, there was no external allurement for me to leave the University position at that time. My good-intentioned advisers were probably concerned about this.

However, they did not know that even though nothing was on the horizon, I had a timeline I must respect. For me, it did not matter where I was heading, so long as my time was up with my credibility intact and my purpose in life was in secure hands.

In the *lead for life* agenda, the leader must stay true to his or her calling, and be constantly mindful or sensitive to the timing surrounding that calling. In my case, any contrary conduct on my part in this circumstance would have been out of place and patently self-defeating. Thus, when the Governing Council approved my request to disengage from the University as Vice Chancellor at its meeting on 4-5 August 2012, an indescribable sense of freedom came over me. I felt light; I felt fulfilled.

In the concluding remarks of my handover note, I stated my view of my finishing as follows.

… A lot has happened in the pioneering

efforts that brought Salem University to where it is today... When we responded to the call to come and pioneer the take-off of the University, hardly did we know what laid ahead. We arrived in Nigeria to confront a tall order in terms of the demand of the University's vision... Like Solomon who asked for wisdom for the mammoth task given to him, we asked God for help to lead and manage as David did: "he (David) shepherded them according to the integrity of his heart, and guided them by the skillfulness of his hands"[26]. God supplied His grace in abundance!

We stayed focused on integrity and skillfulness in all we did, and encouraged other members of the University community to do likewise... We can look back and see the amazing work of the grace of God: "We have

<u>a University</u>", a damn unique one at that! [We achieved this without compromising our character.]

In the same handover notes, we acknowledged the solid help of many stakeholders. The University community, in particular, motivated us with generally undivided loyalty. Alex Haley, the author of *Roots: The Saga of an American Family*, had in his office a picture of a turtle sitting on top of a fence. He said this was to remind him that no one can get to the top (like the turtle) and remain without being helped by people. Likewise, I was constantly mindful of the help that got me into this top seat of responsibility, as in my other previous leadership roles.

Lastly, I said, "like Apostle Paul, 'According to the grace of God which was given to me, as a wise master builder [in our own case, as a favored amateur builder], I have laid the foundation'. It is time for another to build on it". With those notes, which also accounted for all the revenues and expenditures under my watch, I stepped down – no regrets, no machinations! Only freedom; and one's integrity – intact!!

Concluding remarks

Life is replete with situations where not everyone who begins finishes; and not everyone who finishes, finishes well. The reasons for this differing outcomes are quite variegated. For a leader of the *lead for life* mold, though, finishing well is an essential factor in being positioned to deliver upright and high-impact results. To begin with that end in mind, is the first step towards achieving it.

The phrase 'finishing well' may conjure up images of a successful leader sitting on the porch of a nice home not worried about a thing because he had completed active service and achieved great financial success in life. In the *lead for life* discourse, those images would be highly misplaced. Not that it is wrong for leaders to have bank accounts from the legitimate fruits of their lawful labour. No. That is not the point.

The point is that the marks of true leaders bear more fundamentally deeper images of selfless and sacrificial devotion to the general wellbeing of all within the sphere of their influence than the 'comfort' of pinning their embrace of the finishing line on the size of their bank accounts.

One effect of looking for the deeper images of general wellbeing from the beginning is that the leaders free themselves to concentrate their efforts on arriving at the end in dignity. They check to see that their cause is done; choose properly their time of disengagement; maintain their credibility and; like the Mo Ibrahim Award emphasises, retain the joy of making the benefit of their experience and expertise available as opportunities may present them with other public or private roles in their land. They entertain no fears of anything untoward since they 'did not put their hands to evil' while in office.

The *lead for life* leaders are able to get to this position because all along, they:

- maintained a personal devotion to a higher accountability system;

- made themselves life-long learners which meant they could never go out of fashion or relevance;

- manifested Godly character as evidenced by their lifestyles and the impact they had on other lives;

- persevered and saw breakthrough in the myriad of life challenges; and

- developed a sense of destiny, knowing that they were made for something special that would engage them in continuous accomplishment (see Clinton, 2007).

While 'leaders' of a different disposition may go out in a blaze of gory - finishing poorly and leaving a mess in their wake, the *lead for life* leaders go out in a blaze of glory. Like the Biblical Moses did to Joshua, these leaders hand on the baton to the next generation "with dignity, grace, and selfless reflection even [if] in the face of disaster or great failure".

At a critical juncture in Apostle Paul's mission, he said: "… I consider my life worth nothing to me, if only I may finish the race and complete the task the Lord Jesus has given me"[27]. When he got to the end of his assignment, he declared:

> I have fought the good fight, I have finished the race, I have kept the faith: henceforth there is laid up for me the crown of righteousness, which the Lord, the righteous judge, shall give to me at that day...[28]

This is 'dignity - finishing well' par excellence - thoroughly essential in the *lead for life* agenda at the heart of upright and high-impact leadership.

---

[22] Trust Ismamic Forum: "Leadership and followership in Isam (1)", *Daily Trust*, April 3, 2015, p54.

23 See http://en.wikipedia.org/wiki/List_of_current_longest_ruling_non-royal_national_leaders.

[24] 1 Samuel 12:3-4. Holy Bible. King James Version.

25 Stories abound concerning Professors going to extremes lengths to get appointed and/or remain Vice Chancellors. This is not only because of the perceived pecuniary benefits; the position crowns it all for one's academic career. No more heights to conquer after this!

26   Ps 78: 70-72; emphasis added.

27   Acts 20:24, Holy Bible. King James Version.

28   2 Tim. 4:7-8, Holy Bible King James Version.

Conclusion: Where are you?

Is it not a wonder that with the potential for **leadership** which every human being possesses in an overwhelming measure, this phenomenon still remains the scarcest in its manifestation in our world today? At least two issues flow from this question which I took up in the first part of this book.

One, that the 'theory' of only a select few have

the unction for leadership, by birth or 'natural selection' is not one that I subscribe to. And, two, that a lot of what has been paraded under the mantle of leadership - rulers, position holders, organisational chiefs, or power wielders (military, civil, or religious) - like water everywhere, are anything but... The mess or decadence of our world attests to that!

The firmaments are even significantly dimmer when the search turns to upright and positive high-impact leadership. The world has witnessed the rise to power of the 'smart' ones in all the continents. The verdict of history to date is that most of them would fail the leadership character test.

Art of the possible

To the extent that some – no matter how few

- have passed this test, the ***art of the possible*** has been established for that kind of leadership. This is the platform upon which we have set out to enunciate the essentials of a *lead for life* agenda. This agenda has assumed the status of a lifeline for the comity of traumatized nations. And, there is no gainsaying the fact, nor can it be stressed too strongly, that our world needs this kind of leadership seriously.

We have pulled together in this book seven of these core essentials. Aside from the territory that they cover, these essentials also constitute a roadmap for any serious search for, or journey towards, an upright and high-impact leadership. The book is designed and developed in such a way that you can locate where you are on this roadmap and rise to the need of the hour by taking on the *lead for life* agenda.

If you are in the high and mighty position, in whatever context, be aware that many mighty have fallen; and they came to this fate principally because of the failure of character. At certain points in their journeys, they crossed the integrity line into the zone of megalomania and frivolity with damning consequences.

Whether it is Emperor Nero or the President of Enron, the logic of character failure and its attendant trail of 'death' is consistent. And, it leaves the world gasping on a large scale or high-demand level for leaders that respect integrity line. The euphoria that surrounding the March 2015 Presidential elections signaling a change in government in Nigeria is a case in point.

Considering the power of 'interest' in the integrity drive, it is critical that you know and/or commit to selfless interest which prioritises the well-being of **all** over selfish interest and its preoccupation with megalomanic 'me, myself and I'. As we have seen, both types of interest serve as some kind of powerful magnetic force that brings you into a psychological state of engagement, but it is the type you feed or nurture that ultimately determines the kind of leader you become. For instance, history remembers fondly today President Mandela because of the selfless interest that drove his contribution to the rebuilding of South Africa.

Mutually reinforcing to the appreciation of, and commitment to, selfless interest, are the other critical factors or essentials in the *lead for life* agenda as outlined in this book. A vision properly clarified helps leaders to see the future well, so they can (1) get there – in thoughts, words and deeds – before the future arrives, and (2) take others there with positive life-changing experiences.

George Washington saw clearly the USA as a republic governed by virtuous people and "contributing to the uplifting and happiness of the whole world". This drove his leadership of his people. Tegla Loroupe of Kenya saw clearly in the eyes of her mind a peaceful coexistence and socio-economic development of poor and marginalized pastoralists and agro-pastoralists in the Greater Horn of Africa. She remains livid in her pressing on. With clarity comes passion and dedication necessary for a *lead for life* agenda

You need a true compass to get all the stakeholders home safely in accordance with the vision you have so well articulated and modelled. That is what firmly entrenched principles help you to do as a *lead for life* leader. In a decadent world that is crying for redemption, moral rules or upright behavioural frameworks, which is what principles are, would always be your friend as a leader.

Herb Kelleher (CEO of Southwest Airlines), together with his team, has been very strong in setting the values and principles as disclosed in their mission statement that are designed to make Southwest a very relaxed work environment and a business that connects leisurely with its customers.

It is not much use for a leader to see the

vision clearly and to have the right compass in place if no one else buys into, or wants to go somewhere with, that vision. You will be a *lead for life* leader if you go on to communicate the vision to the people so they can own the picture of the future and give their all to it without coercion or manipulation. No factor is more powerful in creating vision-ownership among followers than the leader modeling their passion for the vision.

In this regard, the template of Jesus Christ (the IDEA) remains remarkable till today. Gandhi and Mandela have also left their footprints in this area. For instance, what a statement about the vision of a reconciled South Africa at peace with itself, when Mandela went and took tea with the widow of Verwoerd, the chief architect of apartheid! A vision shared and modeled, is a vision multiplied.

The key litmus test comes down to what you as the leader would do to make the imagined future real. Your competence remains in doubt until you influence your team to produce an edifice befitting the vision. It is by that fact you can sustain your reputation and the loyalty and commitment of others who work with you. Besides having an appropriate interest, vision clarity, softwaring, and buy-in, you must lead centrally (from all sides) in order to get done the turning of vision into reality.

You must not only be visionary, you must be visible – being consistently available to lead by example. It helped me and my team in the pioneering assignment of building Salem University; and it helped Mr Baruti Kafele – a

Principal at Newark Tech High School in Newark, New Jersey, to raise a functional school from a disadvantaged background.

Throughout all this, who you are and what you intend to put forth into your world must be a good and lasting taste of you having touched lives. This is the legacy dimension. The public holiday named after Dr Martin Luther King Jr in the US, the emergence of an African American President (Obama), etc, stand as monuments to what he left behind.

At the finishing line, when you are exiting from the stage, you must get there with your dignity. That means you hand over or hand off the leadership lever timely and in honour. Even if the law or constitution governing your tenure allows you another term, you do what *lead for life* leaders do: step down when you know your time is up and make room for other leaders to take the chance to make their own contribution.

This action brought me freedom, not regret when I did just that at Salem University. Chissano of Mozambique stepped down as President without seeking the allowable third term – to the acclamation of his contemporaries.

For the seven essentials I have outlined in this book to discharge their synergistic force against the pandemic of rapacious misrule, they need to be embodied. Carriers of virtuous leadership, which is the essence of the *lead for life* agenda, must arise in all the facets of life and take their stand against the decadence of their world. Although the need is huge, there is the corresponding huge potential in several people, including you, to meet it head on. So, for me, the preoccupying question is: where are you?

In recognition of the fact that these essentials can be learnt, and that people like you can locate their place on this *lead for life* roadmap, we have established a unique platform, **Omaji Leadership Solutions**, to foster the requisite leadership development. Also, recognising that many people who may already be operating these essentials would be vulnerable to discouragement in their isolation, we have similarly set up the **Virtuous Leaders Development Network** to connect them for mutual support. Information regarding these platforms are available at www.omajileadershipsolutions.

If you are there, or you would like to find out

more about how to locate yourself on this roadmap, please contact us. It is critical that you don't let the world miss out on your incredible potential as a *lead for life* leader.

It is an honour that you have stayed with this book to the end. Take some concrete steps today and be an asset to your world.

References

Cats (2014) "Use your freedom to help ours", http://www.csmonitor.com/World/Making-a-difference/2014/0530/Ursula-Cats-puts-the-concept-educate-one-empower-thousands-to-work.

Campbell, J. (2013) "How Mandela Changed South Africa", http://www.cfr.org/south-africa/mandela-changed-south-africa/p32016.

Cohn, J. and Moran, J. (2011) *Why are we bad at picking good leaders?* Jose Bass, San Franscisco.

Collins, J. (2001) *Good to Great.* Random

House Business Books, London.

Drucker, P. F. (1974) *Management: Tasks, Responsibilities, Practices*. Google Books.

Elkind, P. and McLean, B. (2003) *The Smartest Guys in the Room: The Amazing Rise and Scandalous Fall of Enron*. Viking.

Frieberg, K. and Frieberg, J. (n.d) " Leaders as Value Shapers", Blog post:

http://www.freibergs.com/resources/articles/leadership/leaders-as-value-shapers/

Gandz, J. (2009) "Compelling Visions: Context, Credibility and Collaboration", Ivey Business Journal. Issue: March/April 2009.

Golden, B. (2011) "Self-interest vs. selfish; there is a difference", http://www.presspublications.com/opinionscolumns/146-dare-to-live-without-limits/7386-self-interest-vs-selfish-there-is-a-difference.

Johnson, C. (2003) "Enron's Ethical Collapse: Lessons for Leadership Educators", *Journal of Leadership Education*, Volume 2, Issue 1 –

Summer 2003, pp45-56.

Khan, A. (n.d) "Islamic Leadership Principles: (A Success Model for Everyone and all Times)".
http://www.irfi.org/articles/articles_1401_14 50/islamic_leadership_principles.htm

Kouzes, J. and Posner, B. (2009) "To Lead, Create a Shared Vision", Harvard Business Review, January 2009.

Market Power (2011) "self-interest-vs-selfishness",
http://www.marketpowerblog.com/market_p ower/2011/01/self-interest-vs-selfishness.html.

Maxwell, J. (2007) *The 21 Irrefutable Laws of Leadership. Follow them and people will follow you.* Thomas Nelson. Nashville, USA.

Oestreich, D. (2009) "Is Leadership a Calling?"
http://www.unfoldingleadership.com/blog/? p=585

Omaji, P. (2015) *Audacity of Leading Right: An Odyssey Towards Virtuous Leadership.* Amazon,

Delaware US.

Parker, F. (2013) *Failures of Leadership: History's Worst Rulers and How Their People Suffered For It.* Digital Edition, Kindle.

Paul, A.M. (2013) "The Power of Interest", http://anniemurphypaul.com/2013/11/the-power-of-interest/.

Stanzma, D. (2014) *Leadership: How to lead effectively, efficiently, vocally in a way people will follow.* Kindle Edition.

Stazesky, R.C. "George Washington, Genius in Leadership" . A presentation at a meeting on February 22, 2000 of The George Washington Club, Ltd., Wilmington, Delaware.

Toronto, J.A. (2000) "A Latter-day Saint Perspective on Muhammad", https://www.lds.org/ensign/2000/08/a-latter-day-saint-perspective-on-muhammad?lang=eng#footnote19-20908_000_012

Weed, J. (2013) "Is the human eye irreducibly complex?",

http://skeptoid.com/blog/2013/12/24/is-the-human-eye-irreducibly-complex/.

About the author

Paul Omojo Omaji is a Professor of
Criminology and Vice Chancellor Emeritus.
He trained in Sociology, Criminology, and
Law in Nigeria and Australia. He has
researched, published and lectured in these
fields for about 30 years across Nigeria,
Australia, Singapore, India, South Africa, the
US, Canada, UK, and Sweden.

Professor Omaji has had over 40 years of
community and professional leadership
experiences. These include senior executive

positions in the Australian Government public service where he provided policy advice at ministerial levels and led his teams to deliver successful implementation of government programmes in local communities and overseas countries, including the US, UK, Sweden, Denmark, Austria, the Czech Republic, Italy, and France.

Professor Omaji has also served as an official at all levels in the university system, culminating in his appointment as a pioneer Vice Chancellor of a private University. He is currently the Chief Executive Officer of *Omaji Leadership Solutions* and the *Virtuous Leaders Development Network*.

Professor Omaji has recently released *Audacity of Leading Right: An Odyssey towards Virtuous Leadership*, in which he laid out his very insightful journey in a bold leadership episode in his life.

INDEX